Happy Hour

MIXOLOGY BARTENDER BOOK

INTRODUCTION

The art of mixing cocktails is gaining popularity all the time, which means that more and more people want to learn the secrets of mixing the most popular and tasty cocktails.

Of course, there are no discussions about tastes, but the item you hold in your hands contains a multitude of delicious and world-famous cocktails! With the knowledge about cocktails contained in this book, you will not once surprise your guests and be an expert for them!

First we'll explain what bartending tools and glassware you'll need, then we'll get into cocktails, how to make the 100 most popular cocktails based on vodka, whiskey, rum, gin and tequila.

At the end of the book you will find interesting menu suggestions for popular events such as family barbecue, Christmas, New Year's Eve, and ending with sophisticated: gentlemen's night and ladies party!

HOST PRINCIPLES

————————

1. Try to get recipes for interesting non-alcoholic cocktails and stock up on the ingredients you need. Stock up on softs and serve them all the time. Remember, however, that carbonated drinks combined with alcohol tend to speed up its absorption.

2. Don't make your drinks too strong, and don't try to force your guests to try stronger drinks.

3. Control how much and what kind of alcohol individual guests consume. In the middle of a party they may lose control over the amount of drunk alcohol. Don't let them mix alcohol, because this is the first step towards the end of the party.

4. Provide snacks. Not only will they slow down the absorption of alcohol, but they will increase the quality of your party.

5. Organize games and activities. A party based solely on mass consumption of alcohol never ends up being fun.

6. Serve only top-notch products. It's not just poor alcohol that doubles the hangover. Pseudo juices and colored sodas contain a lot of sugar, which negatively affects your mood the next day.

7. Think for others. It's not easy to talk a drunk person out of having another drink, but your determination can save someone's life.

CONTENTS

INTRODUCTION... 2

HOST PRINCIPLES... 3

BAR TOOLS ... 5

BAR GLASS... 6

BOTTLES... 7

VODKA COCKTAILS.... 8 - 33

WHISKEY COCKTAILS.... 34 - 60

RUM COCKTAILS... 61- 85

TEQUILA COCKTAILS... 86 - 111

GIN COCKTAILS... 112 - 137

MENU RECOMMENDATIONS... 138 - 142

INDEX... 143

BAR TOOLS

Must Have

COCKTAIL SHEAKER   KNIFE   JIGGER

Nice to Have

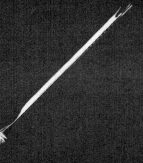

BAR SPOON   ZESTER   STRAINER

BAR GLASS

Must Have

PINT
GLASS

HIGHBALL
GLASS

OLD FASHIONED
GLASS

SHOT
GLASS

COCKTAIL
GLASS

Nice to Have

HURRICANE
GLASS

MARGARITA
GLASS

CHAMPAGNE
GLASS

WINE
GLASS

JAR
GLASS

BOTTLES

Must Have

VODKA   WHISKEY   RUM   TEQUILLA   GIN

Nice to Have

TRIPLE-SEC   GRENADINE   CHAMPAGNE
SWEET VERMOUTH   SIMPLE SYRUP   DIFFRENT SYRUPS
LIME JUICE   BLUE CURACAO   FRUITS
LEMON JUICE   COFFE LIQOUR   STRAWS
BITTERS

COSMOPOLITAN

Cosmopolitan is a classic womanizer that owes its popularity to the TV series Sex and the City. Plus, the drink is tasty and simple! No wonder why it has so many fans! It's also a great option for a party.

Preparation Method

Start by preparing the glass in which you will serve the cocktail. To chill it, put it in the freezer for a few minutes or fill it with ice and set it aside while you prepare the drink. Put ice in a shaker and then pour all the ingredients into it. Using a jigger or a measuring cup, measure out the right amounts to maintain the recipe and the balance of the cocktail. Shake vigorously in a shaker and strain into a chilled cocktail glass (without ice) using a strainer. Garnish the cocktail with the orange peel.

Drink Recipe

40 ml of lime vodka
20 ml Cointreau
20 ml cranberry juice
20 ml lime juice

PORNSTAR MARTINI

The Pornstar Martini is an extremely sumptuous cocktail with a tropical flavor. A wonderfully sweet vanilla aroma combined with an exotic and refreshing passion fruit mousse enhanced with vodka and finished with bubbles from Prosseco

Preparation Method

Slit open the passion fruit and scoop out the pulp with a spoon, which you then put into a shaker (if you are using fresh passion fruit - for the purée just pour the appropriate amount into the shaker). Add all ingredients except champagne, shake with ice and pour into a glass. Serve the champagne separately from the drink, in a shot glass. It is important to inform the drinker that the two parts of the drink should be drunk separately. Garnish with half a passion fruit.

Drink Recipe

60 ml Vanilla vodka
60 ml Champagne brut
15 ml Passion fruit puree
15 ml Lime juice
15 ml Vanilla sugar syrup
15 ml Passoa

VODKA SOUR

If instead of a quick weightlessness you prefer to spend time with a cocktail that is firstly very simple to prepare and secondly the taste of alcohol is almost undetectable, then this is a good choice.

Preparation Method

If you choose a recipe with protein, pour the protein into the shaker without ice and shake vigorously to aerate it. Add ice and the rest of the ingredients and shake vigorously. Pour into a whiskey glass topped up with ice. Garnish with a lime wedge or fresh mint.

Drink Recipe

50 ml vodka
20 ml of lemon juice
10 ml of sugar syrup
20 ml egg white - optional

SEX ON THE BEACH

It is a drink with a very hot name, pleasant and sweet taste and is refreshing and perfect for hot summer days.

Preparation Method

Pour vodka, orange juice and peach liqueur into a shaker filled with ice. Shake vigorously. Pour the contents of the shaker into a tall glass filled with ice cubes. Finally, add cranberry juice to the glass. For a better effect, decorate the drink with fruit slices. Since you mustn't let sex be boring, we've put together the following suggestions for variety. "Royal Sex on the Beach" - in the above recipe, use Chambord liqueur in place of peach liqueur and pineapple juice in place of orange juice. "Torrid Sex on the Beach" - in place of peach liqueur, give coconut liqueur. "Sex on Fire" - in place of vodka, we use cinnamon whiskey.

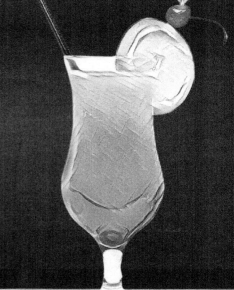

Drink Recipe

40 ml vodka
20 ml peach liqueur
60 ml of orange juice
60 ml cranberry juice

LONG ISLAND ICE TEA

The Long Island Iced Tea cocktail was first served in the late 1970s by a bartender from the town of Babylon, Long Island. The most popular version of the cocktail is composed of equal parts of ingredients (vodka, gin, tequila, rum and triple sec)

Preparation Method

Start by preparing the glass in which you will serve the cocktail. To chill it, put it in the freezer for a few minutes or fill it with ice and set it aside while you prepare the drink. Put ice in a shaker and then pour all the ingredients into it. Using a jigger or a measuring cup, measure out the right amounts to maintain the recipe and the balance of the cocktail. Shake vigorously in a shaker and strain into a chilled cocktail glass (without ice) using a strainer. Garnish the cocktail with the orange peel.

Drink Recipe

20 ml of pure vodka
20 ml gin
20 ml of pale rum
20 ml silver tequila
20 ml cointreau
20 ml lime juice
20 ml lemon juice
20 ml of sugar syrup
40 ml cola

WHITE RUSSIAN

White Russian It is a combination of vodka, coffee liqueur and cream and has been in the canon of classic cocktails for years. And how did the drink get its name? Admittedly, the cocktail does not originate from Russia, but it contains alcohol that is very associated with it - it is pure vodka.

Preparation Method

Put some ice in a shaker, then pour in all the ingredients one by one and shake. Using a bar strainer into a chilled low glass, strain the cocktail from the shaker or jar. The last thing you need to do is add a few fresh ice cubes to the glass.

Drink Recipe

40 ml of pure vodka
20 ml coffee liqueur
20 ml cream

CAIPIROSCA

Caipiriosca is a close relative of the Brazilian cocktail Caipirinha. The only difference between the two is the alcohol that forms the base of the drink. The Caipirinha is made with cachaça, a traditional Brazilian alcohol made from sugar cane juice. The Caipiriosca is made up of pure vodka.

Preparation Method

Prepare a glass in which to serve the cocktail, then place a lime in it and pour in the sugar syrup. Muddle the lime and the sugar syrup, then add the crushed ice and pour the vodka. Stir gently with a barman's spoon and top up with crushed ice again.

Drink Recipe

40 ml of pure vodka
20 ml of sugar syrup
2 lime quarters

BLACK RUSSIAN

Black Russian was created around 1950 by a bartender Gustave Tops working in Metropole Hotel in Brussels. It is said that one of the guests at that time and a fan of Black Russian was the ambassador of the United States Pearl Mesta.

Preparation Method

A simple drink consisting of only two ingredients. These are pure vodka and Mexican coffee liqueur Kahlua mixed with ice and served in a low glass.

Drink Recipe

40 ml of pure vodka
20 ml coffee liqueur

METROPOLITAN

This classic looking cocktail from 1990 is actually the lesser known brother of the great "Cosmopolitan". Made more interesting with currant vodka, it is a very interesting alternative for fans of the drink from "Sex in the City".

Preparation Method

Start by preparing the glass in which you will serve the cocktail. Fill it with ice and set aside for a few minutes, or put it in the freezer while you prepare the cocktail. Put ice in a shaker and then pour in all the ingredients. Stir vigorously and strain into a chilled cocktail glass. Use orange peel as a garnish.

Drink Recipe

40 ml currant vodka
10 ml cointreau
40 ml cranberry juice
10 ml lime juice

BLOODY MARY

A Bloody Mary, of course! This drink is a delicious option for lazy, hungover breakfasts with friends. The coolest thing about it is that you can combine with additives according to your own preferences.

Preparation Method

Pour 40 ml of vodka and 80 ml of tomato juice into a shaker. Then add a pinch of salt, some freshly ground pepper, a splash of Worcester sauce, 2-3 drops of Tabasco and half a teaspoon of simple horseradish. Fill the shaker with ice cubes and stir everything with a bartender's spoon. Take a cocktail glass and gently strain the water from the melted ice, top up with ice cubes and use a bar strainer to strain the contents of the shaker into the glass. Top up the drink with tomato juice. Top with the blue cheese and garnish with fresh basil.

Drink Recipe

40 ml vodka
100 ml tomato juice
pinch of salt
freshly ground pepper
worcester sauce
tabasco
horseradish

VODKA COLLINS

The Vodka Collins cocktail is also known as the Joe Collins. In one sentence, it is an easy to prepare, boozy lemonade. The composition is very similar to the classic Tom Collins drink, except that here instead of gin there is pure vodka.

Preparation Method

Pour vodka, lime juice, lemon juice and sugar syrup into a shaker. Shake the ingredients in a shaker and pour the cocktail into a tall glass filled with ice. Then fill the glass with sparkling water. Use a quarter lime as a garnish, enjoy!

Drink Recipe

60 ml of pure vodka
80 ml sparkling water
10 ml of lime juice
10 ml of lemon juice
20 ml of sugar syrup

KAMIKADZE SHOT

Memories especially at a club party. These sweet and sour classics are similar in taste to a classic margarita.

Preparation Method

First, prepare a crust, which is a striking and flavorful garnish for the rim of the glass. Take half a lemon and wet the rim of the glass with it. Then sprinkle some citric acid on the dish and "soak" the rim of the glass in it. Squeeze 40 ml of lemon juice into the glass. Set aside. Pour 40 ml of vodka, 40 ml of blue Curaçao and 40 ml of lemon juice into a shaker, fill with ice cubes and shake thoroughly. Using a bar strainer, strain the contents of the glass into pre-decorated glasses.

Drink Recipe

40 ml vodka
40 ml blue curacao
40 ml lemon juice
For decoration:
half a lemon

DIRTY DANCING

Dirty Dancing cocktail. Its catchy name causes that on the Internet circulate a lot of more or less different recipes of drinks that bear the name Dirty Dancing.

Preparation Method

Start by preparing the glass in which you will serve the cocktail. To chill it, put it in the freezer for a few minutes or fill it with ice and set it aside while you prepare the drink. Put ice in a shaker and then pour all the ingredients into it. Using a jigger or a measuring cup, measure out the right amounts to maintain the recipe and the balance of the cocktail. Shake vigorously in a shaker and strain into a chilled cocktail glass (without ice) using a strainer. Garnish the cocktail with the orange peel.

Drink Recipe

20 ml gin
20 ml white rum
10 ml vodka
70 ml passion fruit juice
70 ml orange juice
25 ml strawberry syrup
5 ml lime juice

BUCKET LIST

Bucket list is a honey and herb vodka based cocktail. It is quite simple, and the main fiddle here is the herbal liqueur, which makes this drink has a very interesting and attractive aroma. We associate it very much with spring.

Preparation Method

Start by preparing the glass in which you will serve the cocktail. Fill it with ice and set aside for a few minutes or put it in the freezer while you prepare the cocktail.
Put ice in a shaker and then pour in all the ingredients. Stir vigorously and strain into a chilled cocktail glass. Use a sprig of rosemary as a garnish.

Drink Recipe

40 ml vodka
20 ml Genepi liqueur
20 ml lemon juice
20 ml honey syrup

VESPER MARTINI

James Bond's favorite drink under the famous shaken, not stirred. How does the Vesper differ from the classic Martini? First, our cocktail will contain vodka, not just gin (as in the Dry Martini). The second difference is the preparation - the Vesper Martini is shaken in a shaker and not just stirred.

Preparation Method

Prepare the glass in which you will serve the cocktail - fill with ice to chill and leave it while you prepare the drink, or place in the freezer for a few minutes. Pour all ingredients into the prepared shaker with ice and shake. Strain the drink prepared this way using a bartender's strainer into a chilled glass. The last step to the perfect cocktail is the garnish. Garnish your drink with lemon zest.

Drink Recipe

20 ml of pure vodka
60 ml gin
10 ml Lillet blanc

California Lemonade is a citrusy cocktail based on vodka, gin and brandy. Despite a considerable amount of alcohol it is really cool. Although in our opinion lemonade is too delicate a term for this killer.

Preparation Method

Pour all ingredients into prepared shaker with ice and shake. Pour into a tall glass. Time for the last step - garnish! Garnish our cocktail with lemon peel.

Drink Recipe

40 ml clear vodka
40 ml gin
40 ml brandy
80 ml orange juice
20 ml lime juice
20 ml Grenadine

RAFAELLO

_____

The dominant flavors we discover in Rafaello are coconut, almond, chocolate, coffee, vanilla.

Preparation Method

Shake all ingredients in a shaker filled with ice. Strain into a glass garnished with coconut shavings.

Drink Recipe

40 ml coconut liqueur
30 ml Irish Cream such
as Bailey's or Carolan's
30 ml condensed milk
20 ml amaretto liqueur

NIAGARA FALLS

The combination of citrus and ginger makes Niagara Falls taste, look and feel refreshing.

Preparation Method

Pour the vodka, grand marnier and lemon juice into a shaker. Then shake the whole thing with ice and pour into a chilled glass. Finally pour the ginger ale. Use orange segments as a garnish.

Drink Recipe

40 ml vodka
40 ml Grand Marnier liqueur
80 ml Ginger Ale
20 ml of lemon juice
10 ml sugar syrup

KILLER PUNCH

Killer Punch is not a killer! Especially in taste, it is delicate, sweet and fruity. Its flavors are perfectly balanced and the color is noticeable from a distance. Try it for yourself.

Preparation Method

Killer Punch is composed directly in a tall glass. Just pour fresh ice cubes into it, pour all ingredients and stir. At the end use a piece of lime for decoration and you're done. Nothing difficult, right?

Drink Recipe

40 ml vodka
20 ml melon liqueur
20 ml almond liqueur
80 ml cranberry juice
20 ml of lime juice

CHILL OUT MARTINI

The Chill Out Martini drink certainly belongs to the genre of inconspicuous, but deadly. This is largely due to the softness of the cocktail and its creamy texture, which contrasts with the relatively high alcohol concentration.

Preparation Method

Fill a cocktail glass with ice and set aside while you prepare the drink, or place in the freezer for a few minutes to chill. Using a measuring cup, measure the exact amounts of ingredients, then pour them into a shaker with ice and shake vigorously. Strain the cocktail (without ice) into a glass and garnish with a piece of pineapple.

Drink Recipe

20 ml tangerine vodka
20 ml irish cream
20 ml malibu
20 ml orange juice

HAND GRANADE

A combination of gin, white rum, vodka, melon liqueur and pineapple juice, this 1984 cocktail was created by the then owners of the Tropical Isle bar. Interestingly, since 1992, the cocktail has been served in a vessel that resembles a hand grenade.

Preparation Method

Before you pour your cocktail into the glass in which you will serve it, put a few ice cubes in it to chill it. Then, pour all the ingredients into a shaker and shake the whole thing with a few ice cubes. Pour the contents of the shaker into the chilled glass and garnish with a lime wedge. Done! It may not be explosive, but it is very tasty.

Drink Recipe

30 ml Gin
30 ml White rum
30 ml Vodka
40 ml Melon liqueur
40 ml Pineapple juicel

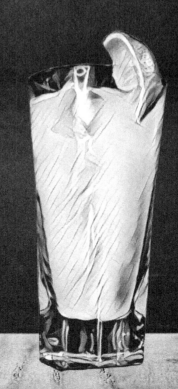

Madroska is the apple sister of the Madras cocktail. It is equally versatile, refreshing and simple to make. Be sure to let us know which sibling appeals more to your taste!

Preparation Method

We compose the Madrosca just like the Brother - directly in a tall glass. Fill it with ice cubes and then pour in all the ingredients. Using a jigger or kitchen measuring cup, we measure out the right amounts, which allows us to maintain the correct recipe and balance the taste of the cocktail. Gently mix the cocktail. Finally, garnish with an orange segments. Ready

Drink Recipe

40 ml vodka clear
40 ml orange juice
40 ml cranberry juice
60 ml apple juice

PORTOFINO

Beautiful marina, exclusive boutiques, expensive hotels and stunning views. One of the most beautiful and also the most expensive towns on the Italian Riviera is called Portofino. Here is an exclusive drink of Portofino.

Preparation Method

Compose all ingredients in order in a tall glass filled with ice. Stir gently. Garnish with a piece of grapefruit.

Drink Recipe

10 ml Campari
40 ml red grapefruit juice
60 ml tonic

SCREAMING ORGASM

Screaming Orgasm is a typical dessert cocktail from the 80s, which enjoys its fame mainly due to good marketing. It is definitely not for those who care about their diet

Preparation Method

Fill a hurricane type glass with crushed ice. Put a few ice cubes in a shaker and pour in all the ingredients in equal proportions. Shake it all up and, using a bar strainer, strain the contents of the shaker into the prepared glass. Garnish the cocktail with grated chocolate.

Drink Recipe

20 ml Vodka
20 ml Coffee liqueur
20 ml Almond liqueur
20 ml Irish cream
20 ml Cream

POLISH MARTINI

Bison Vodka, krupnik and apple juice in one glass is a reference to Polish culture. If this combination is too dry for you, you can optionally add honey liqueur of your choice.

Preparation Method

Start by chilling the glass in which you will serve the cocktail - fill it with ice and set aside while you prepare the cocktail or put it in the freezer for a few minutes. Next, prepare a shaker and pour the ice into it. Using a kitchen brand, measure the exact amounts of all ingredients and pour them into the shaker. Shake vigorously and strain without ice into a chilled glass. Garnish the cocktail with a lemon peel. Cheers!

Drink Recipe

30 ml - Bison Vodka
30 ml - krupnik (Vodka)
30 ml - apple juice

WHISKEY SOUR

One of the most popular whiskey-based drinks. In addition to the basic ingredients, it is also very popular to add chicken protein and a few drops of Angostura Bitter. In this case, you need to shake the cocktail very hard so that the protein is properly whipped. For this purpose, a preparation technique called "dry shake" is often used when making Whiskey Sour. This method involves shaking all the ingredients without ice, and then shaking again with ice.

Preparation Method

Put ice cubes into a shaker. Then pour whiskey, sugar syrup and lemon juice. Stir everything vigorously. Pour the finished drink into a low glass filled with ice cubes. Decorate with a slice or a piece of lemon before serving

Drink Recipe

40 ml whiskey
20 ml of lemon juice
10 ml of sugar syrup

OLD FASHIONED

One of the most classic - drinks on the globe - Old Fashioned. It is a dry drink based on whiskey or bourbon with a little sugar (some use sugar cubes), bitters (angostura), soda water and a large ice cube.

Preparation Method

Stir all ingredients with a bar spoon in a glass, slowly adding more ice cubes. Use a cocktail cherry and orange peel as garnish.

Drink Recipe

60 ml American bourbon whiskey
10 ml sugar syrup
2 dashes of angostura

GODFATHER

It is a very simple drink to prepare, as it contains only two ingredients: scotch whisky and amaretto liqueur. The Godfather is also not a technically difficult drink, not does it require advanced tools in its use.

Preparation Method

All you need to do is pour, in order, 40 ml of Scotch whisky and 20 ml of amaretto liqueur into a low glass with ice. Then mix the ingredients thoroughly, and our Godfather is ready.

Drink Recipe

40 ml Scotch whisky
20 ml amaretto liqueur

MANHATTAN

This cocktail was first made at a Manhattan Club party in 1874. It was hosted by Jennie Churchill, the American mother of Winston Churchill.

Preparation Method

Stir all ingredients in a shaker with ice and strain into a chilled glass. Use a cocktail cherry as garnish.

Drink Recipe

60 ml American bourbon whiskey
30 ml sweet vermouth
2 dashes of angostura

MONTREAL

This aromatic cocktail is a combination of juniper, a bittersweet liqueur straight from Italy, rye whiskey, and French honey-herb liqueur. On the one hand, confusion with confusion, on the other, a good balance of flavors and aromas. Montreal is an excellent option to serve as an aperitif.

Preparation Method

Pour the proper amounts of ingredients into a shaker filled with ice. A jigger will help you measure out the exact amounts. Shake the ingredients and, using a bartender's strainer, strain into a chilled glass (without ice). Garnish the cocktail with grapefruit peel.

Drink Recipe

30 ml Gin
30 ml Rye whiskey
30 ml Aperol
30 ml Suze gentian
liqueur

NEW YORKER

Very simple, very elegant, very American, and thanks to the perfect composition of ingredients it maintains a balanced balance of flavors. One thing is certain - the New Yorker cocktail is a real treat for gourmets of American bourbon whiskey!

Preparation Method

The first step is to chill the glass in which you will serve the cocktail - fill it with ice or put it in the freezer for a few minutes. Put some ice in a shaker, then pour in all the ingredients one by one and shake. Using a bar strainer, strain the cocktail from the shaker into the chilled glass. The last thing you need to do is garnish the cocktail with orange peel... and you're done!

Drink Recipe

40 ml American bourbon whiskey
20 ml of lemon juice
10 ml sugar syrup
10 ml of grenadine

IRISH BOULEVARDIER

This is another cocktail that will appeal to Negroni lovers. Simplicity and bitterness are definitely characteristics of this type of drink.

Preparation Method

Put a few ice cubes in a low glass, then pour in equal amounts of ingredients in order. Gently stir the whole thing and garnish with some orange zest. Done! Enjoy!

Drink Recipe

40 ml Irish blended whiskey
40 ml Campari
40 ml sweet vermouth

LYNCHBURG LEMONADE

A classic cocktail from Jack Daniels. A refreshing and citrusy drink based on whisky. In our opinion a fantastic alcoholic alternative to lemonade. Depending on your preference, you can also add Angostura bitters to the classic recipe. It will turn up the flavor and aroma of the cocktail.

Preparation Method

Shake all ingredients except lemonade in a shaker. Then pour everything into a tall glass. Finally pour in the lemonade. Use a piece of lemon as a garnish. Tip: Keep in mind that adding the exact amounts of ingredients will allow you to maintain the original recipe of the cocktail and thus the perfect balance of flavors in the Lynchburg Lemonade drink.

Drink Recipe

40 ml American Tennessee whiskey
20 ml Cointreau triple sec
100 ml lemonade
10 ml lime juice
10 ml lemon juice
10 ml sugar syrup

TENNESSEE FIRE BEER

Fiery shots made with a combination of Jack Fire and light beer! Great to start the party!

Preparation Method

Pour 50ml of Jack Daniel's Tenneesse Fire and 50ml of pale lager into a shaker. 2. Top up the shaker with ice and shake thoroughly. Using a bar strainer, strain the contents of the glass into three shot glasses. 4. For extra flavor, you can heat up some cinnamon powder and sprinkle it on top of the drink. Enjoy!

Drink Recipe

50ml Jack Daniel's
Tennessee Fire
50 ml pale lager
For decoration:
cinnamon powder

KENTUCKY COLONEL

The Colonel is a cocktail not just for bourbon lovers. This drink is mild and pleasant in taste due to the combination of whiskey and fruit. It will be perfect for a summer afternoon.

Preparation Method

Shake all ingredients in a shaker and strain contents into a tall glass filled with ice. Garnish with a slice of pineapple. If you have canned pineapple on hand, use a half or quarter slice; if you have fresh pineapple, it's best to cut off a small piece and garnish.

Drink Recipe

40 ml American bourbon whiskey
20 ml apricot liqueur
60 ml pineapple juice
10 ml lemon juice

BURBON COOKIE

Exotic and dessert-y? Be sure to try Bourbon Cookie! This combination may seem unusual at first, but we guarantee that Bourbon Cookie will become a favorite of many of you.

Preparation Method

Start by chilling the glass in which you will serve the cocktail - fill it with ice and leave it for a few minutes or place it in the freezer while you prepare the cocktail. Put ice in a shaker and then pour the carefully measured drink ingredients. Shake vigorously for about 10-15 seconds and strain the cocktail (without ice) into a chilled glass. Decorate Bourbon Cookie with cinnamon sprinkled on top. Enjoy!

Drink Recipe

40 ml American bourbon whiskey
10 ml passion fruit liqueur
10 ml caramel/toffee liqueur
20 ml cream

AGGRAVATION

Aggravation defiantly has nothing to do with aggravation, unless you want to drink it to improve your mood. Preferably in the company of female friends during #girlsnight. It is a typically ladylike cocktail based on whisky. The addition of coffee liqueur, cream and sugar syrup makes it velvety and melt in your mouth.

Preparation Method

Start by preparing the glass in which you will serve the cocktail - fill it with ice to chill it and set aside for a few minutes or place it in the freezer while you prepare the cocktail. Put ice in a shaker and then pour the carefully measured ingredients. Shake vigorously for about 10-15 seconds and strain (without ice) into a chilled glass. Grate fresh nutmeg on top of the cocktail and... done!

Drink Recipe

40 ml scotch blended whisky
20 ml coffee liqueur
20 ml cream
10 ml sugar syrup

IRISH COFFE

Irish coffee is probably the most famous drink served hot. Its undoubted advantages are taste, warming properties and the ease, due to the simple recipe, of preparation at home.

Preparation Method

Heat a cup or glass with ears by pouring in boiling water. Pour out the contents. Then pour in all the ingredients except the cream and stir. Shake the cream in a small jar or squeeze bottle until whipped. Gently spoon the cream over the top of the mug. Garnish with 3 coffee beans.

Drink Recipe

30 ml Irish whiskey
60 ml of freshly brewed coffee
15 ml sugar syrup
30 ml cream (18%)

TENNESSEE ICED TEA

After tasting this cocktail, we don't get what we expected - it's certainly no ordinary iced tea on JackDaniels. This is another version of its famous predecessor: Island Iced Tea.

Preparation Method

Pour all ingredients (except cola!) into a shaker and shake vigorously for about 10-15 seconds. Pour the whole thing into a tall school filled with fresh ice, and top it off with cola. The final step to the perfect cocktail is garnish! Use a piece of lemon as a garnish... and you're done! Enjoy!

Drink Recipe

40 ml American Tennessee whiskey
15 ml light rum
15 ml vodka
15 ml Cointreau triple sec
20 ml lemon juice
10 ml sugar syrup
40 ml cola

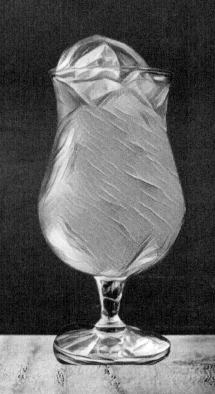

PENICILLIN

This famous 2005 cocktail was created by Sam Ross at New York's Milk & Honey. The combination of butterscotch, ginger, honey and lemon is a perfect suggestion for colder days. It may not cure, but it will surely make your moment more pleasant.

Preparation Method

In the bottom of a shaker, squeeze the fresh ginger until juiced. Then add a few ice cubes and pour in the remaining ingredients. Shake vigorously and strain into a low glass filled with fresh ice using a bar strainer. Enjoy!

Drink Recipe

50 ml Scotch whisky
30 ml lemon juice
15 ml honey
piece of ginger

ADAM&EVE

This cocktail is a nod to the forbidden fruit. It is an exquisite drink with an unobvious taste. We create it on a base of American Bourbon Whisky and Galliano, which makes in this cocktail strongly noticeable herbal aromas. The whole is complemented by sugar syrup and Angostura Bitters.

Preparation Method

Put ice in a shaker and then, using a jigger, carefully measure and pour all the ingredients. Shake vigorously and pour the cocktail into a low glass. Use lemon peel as a garnish. Don't be afraid to sin!

Drink Recipe

40 ml American Bourbon Whisky
10 ml Galliano Liqueur
10 ml sugar syrup
3 dash Angostura Bitter

KENTUCKY TEA

Kentucky Tea, despite appearances, has nothing to do with tea. Only the color of the drink may be associated with it. However, the recipe for this cocktail combines American bourbon, the orange aromas of cointreau, the sharp ginger flavor of Ginger ale, and lime juice to create the perfect, refreshing drink for summer.

Preparation Method

Pour all ingredients (except Ginger ale!) into a shaker and shake vigorously for about 10-15 seconds. Pour the whole thing into a tall school filled with fresh ice, then top off with Ginger ale. The final step to the perfect cocktail is garnish! Use a lime wedge as a garnish... and you're done!

Drink Recipe

40 ml whiskey
20 ml Cointreau
20 ml of lime juice
10 ml sugar syrup
100 ml Ginger Ale

CUNNINGHAM MARTINI

This interesting variation on Blood and Sand swaps sweet vermouth for herbal liqueur and lemon juice. This combination makes the Cunningham Martini fresh, even more citrusy and refreshing. If you are a fan of the original version of the cocktail, you will surely enjoy this one as well.

Preparation Method

Start by preparing the glass in which you will serve the cocktail. To chill it, put it in the freezer for a few minutes or fill it with ice and set it aside while you prepare the drink. Put ice in a shaker and then pour all the ingredients into it. With the help of a jigger, measure out the right quantities to keep the recipe and the balance of the cocktail. Shake vigorously in a shaker and strain into a chilled cocktail glass (without ice) using a strainer. Finally, garnish the cocktail with orange peel and a cherry and you're done!

Drink Recipe

60 ml Scotch blended whisky
20 ml lemon juice
20 ml Red orange juice
20 ml Benedictine
20 ml cherry liqueur

PURSUIT OF HAPPINESS

We are not sure if you will find happiness with this cocktail, however, it will definitely make your moment more pleasant. Especially if you are a fan of Negroni on scotch. The Pursuit of Happiness will work both as an aperitif and as a digestif.

Preparation Method

Start by preparing a low glass in which to serve the drink. Fill it with ice and set aside to chill or place in the freezer while you prepare the cocktail. Pour ice into a shaker, then pour in the ingredients and stir thoroughly. Strain into a chilled glass filled with fresh ice. The last step to a perfect cocktail is garnish! A bunch of mint is a great garnish. Good luck!

Drink Recipe

40 ml blended Scotch whisky
20 ml banana liqueur
15 ml Campari

STILETTO

If you are looking for an intensely fruity cocktail - Stiletto is just for you! Almond liqueur combined with cranberry juice and sugar syrup gives our drink sweetness and fruity aroma. The acidity of the lime juice keeps the balance and the American Tennessee whiskey casually appears in the background of the range of flavors, giving shape to the whole.

Preparation Method

Start by preparing your shaker - fill it with ice and use a jigger or kitchen measuring cup to measure out the exact amounts of ingredients one by one. Then pour the ingredients into the shaker and shake vigorously. Pour the cocktail into a tall glass. Garnish the drink with a quarter of a lime. A very simple and very tasty recipe!

Drink Recipe

40 ml Tennessee whiskey
20 ml almond liqueur
100 ml cranberry juice
20 ml lime juice
10 ml sugar syrup

WHISKY MAC

The combination of Scotch with green ginger wine was named Whisky Macdonald in honor of Colonel Hector Macdonald. It is also often found in the drink menu in the shortened form "Whisky Mac". This simple combination is perfect for warming up on winter evenings

Preparation Method

The cocktail itself is very simple in both composition and preparation. All you have to do is put a few ice cubes in a low glass, then pour in the proper amounts of ingredients and stir gently. Nothing too difficult, right?

Drink Recipe

60 ml Scotch Whisky
40 ml Green ginger wine

FLYING SCOTSMAN

This aromatic "Rob Roy" is named after a steam locomotive made in 1923. Highly recommended for those who find solo scotch too dry . The combination with vermouth, angostura and sugar syrup is much easier to drink.

Preparation Method

The cocktail is served in a low, chilled glass, so start by filling the glass with ice or putting it in the freezer for a few minutes. Then prepare a shaker and pour in all the ingredients. Stir thoroughly and pour into a low glass filled with fresh ice. Garnish with orange peel.

Drink Recipe

40 ml Scotch blended whisky
40 ml Ssweet vermouth
5 ml Sugar syrup
Angostura - 3 dashes

ALGONQUIN

Caramel Manhattan was composed in 2002 in London. Bourbon, sweet vermouth, toffee liqueur and pineapple juice. Sounds delicious, doesn't it? These very ingredients come together in an interestingly constructed cocktail with many layers of flavors. We definitely recommend trying it when you feel like something sweet. It will be a great alternative to dessert.

Preparation Method

Pour the measured ingredients into a shaker. Shake vigorously for about 10-15 seconds, then strain over ice into a chilled glass. Garnish with a piece of pineapple.

Drink Recipe

40 ml American bourbon whiskey -
10 ml sweet vermouth
20 ml toffee liqueur
20 ml pineapple juice
Peychaud's bitter - 2 dashes

BRAINSTORM

This elegant cocktail is a dry version of the popular Manhattan, further enhanced with herbal notes. Irish whiskey and Benedictine work well together, and the dry vermouth balances them perfectly. As the name suggests, this is a full-bodied brainstorm on flavor.

Preparation Method

Prepare a cocktail glass. Chill the glass itself in the freezer or fill with ice. Pour all ingredients into a shaker with ice, stir and strain into the chilled glass. Pour into the glass and finish the cocktail using orange zest.

Drink Recipe

60 ml Irish blended whiskey
20 ml dry vermouth
20 ml Benedictine

RUSTY NAIL

The Rusty Nail is a cocktail that originated in 1940s Hawaii. All you need to make this flavorful cocktail is your favorite scotch and drambuie. A combination with strong whiskey and honey and herbal notes.

Preparation Method

Put a few ice cubes in a low glass, then pour in the ingredients and stir gently. You can change the proportions slightly depending on your preference. Nothing difficult, right?

Drink Recipe

60 ml Scotch Blended Whisky
30 ml Drambuie

CUBA LIBRE

The Cuba Libre is one of the most famous classic drinks, and it doesn't look like that will change as long as the world is the world and Coca Cola is Coca Cola.

Preparation Method

Squeeze a medium sized lionfish into a glass, then give it an extra squeeze with a muddler so that it gives off the oils contained in the top rind. Then add plenty of ice, light rum and Coca Cola.

Drink Recipe

40 ml of pale rum
120 ml Coca Cola
juice of 1/4 lime

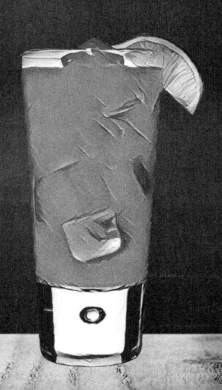

CAIPIRINHA

Tasty and easy to prepare, Caipirinha is Brazil's national alcoholic cocktail. It consists of cachaça (Brazilian alcohol made from fresh sugar cane juice), lime, and sugar syrup.

Preparation Method

In the glass in which you will serve the cocktail, put the lime and pour the sugar syrup. Muddle everything and add crushed ice. Then pour the cachaca and stir gently with a barman's spoon. Top up with crushed ice again... and you're done! Enjoy

Drink Recipe

40 ml of cachaca
20 ml of sugar syrup
2 lime quarters

MOJITO

Mojito is another uncomplicated cocktail that requires few ingredients to prepare: rum, mint, lime, sugar and soda water. It is rare to find a drink as refreshing as the mojito. This composition was developed in Cuba and around 1980s it became extremely popular all over the world.

Preparation Method

Prepare the lime: wash it thoroughly and scald in boiling water. Then gently squeeze it. Stand it upright on a flat part and cut in half. Remove the backbone of the lime (it contains a lot of bitterness). Then cut the lime into smaller pieces. Place the lime segments in a tall glass, add 2-3 teaspoons of sugar and muddle. Add the mint leaves and gently muddle again. Fill the glass with crushed ice. Add 40 ml of rum. Stir everything with a barman's spoon. Add crushed ice again and top up with sparkling water.

Drink Recipe

40 ml of pale rum
20 ml of sugar syrup
2 lime quarters
6 mint leaves
sparkling water

DAIQUIRI

a popular alcoholic cocktail based on white rum, sugar syrup and lime juice. The name, according to some, comes from the language of the Taino Indians who once lived in the Caribbean.

Preparation Method

Mix ingredients in a shaker with ice and then pour into a cocktail glass.

Drink Recipe

60 ml of white rum
22 ml of sugar syrup
30 ml of lime juice

ACAPULCO

Acapulco is a crisp cocktail made with a base of rum and tequila. It is very light and fruity. Everyone will enjoy it, especially on hot days. Not without reason it is named after a hot city in Mexico. Especially recommended for tequila fans.

Preparation Method

Fill a shaker with ice and pour all the ingredients into it. Shake all ingredients vigorously in a shaker and then, using a bar strainer, strain into a tall glass filled with fresh ice. The final step to the perfect cocktail is the garnish! In our cocktail the garnish will be a pineapple chunk. Nothing difficult, right?

Drink Recipe

40 ml white rum
40 ml silver tequila
80 ml pineapple juice
40 ml of grapefruit juice
20 ml of sugar syrup

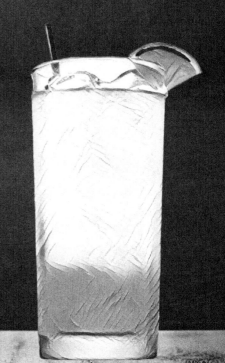

JUNGLE JUICE

Jungle Juice is another tasty candidate, for an exotic cocktail. The pillars of this cocktail are vodka, white rum and cointreau liqueur. Its complement is a real juice jungle. In this one drink you will find lime juice, orange juice, cranberry juice and pineapple juice.

Preparation Method

Put the cocktail glass in the freezer for a few minutes or fill it with ice and set aside to chill. Put ice in a shaker, pour in the right quantities of vodka, white rum, orange juice and cointreau and shake vigorously. Pour the cocktail into a chilled cocktail glass. Use a piece of orange as a garnish.

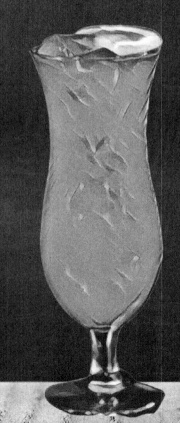

Drink Recipe

30 ml vodka
30 ml white rum
10 ml of Cointreau
30 ml of orange juice
30 ml cranberry juice
30 ml pineapple juice
20 ml lime juice
10 ml sugar syrup

SUNSHINE COCKTAIL

An exceptionally salty cocktail. The combination of dark rum, dry vermouth, pineapple juice and grenadine is very satisfying. It will make you move to the hot Florida. If you taste it during the Polish winter, raise a toast to the sun!

Preparation Method

Prepare a glass and put a few ice cubes in it to chill. Pour all the ingredients into a shaker with ice and shake. Strain the cocktail through a bar strainer into the chilled glass. Garnish with a slice of pineapple. Have a sunny day!

Drink Recipe

30 ml of dark rum
30 ml dry vermouth
30 ml pineapple juice
5 ml Grenadine

PINA COLADA

Pina Colada is a tropical drink usually associated with vacations in warm countries. We often sip this cocktail on the beach, by the sea, on hot days off from work.

Preparation Method

Put all ingredients except ice into a blender and blend thoroughly. Add crushed ice and blend again for a moment (about 3 seconds).Pour into goblets and serve.

Drink Recipe

40 ml of rum
40 ml coconut milk
5 slices of canned pineapple
Crushed ice (approx. half a cup)

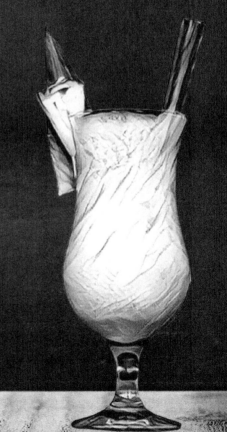

MAI TAI

Acapulco is a crisp cocktail made with a base of rum and tequila. It is very light and fruity. Everyone will enjoy it, especially on hot days. Not without reason it is named after a hot city in Mexico. Especially recommended for tequila fans.

Preparation Method

The very name of the cocktail indicates that we are sure to enjoy it - Maita'i in Tahitian simply means good. We may encounter different spellings, but it will always be the same, delicious rum-based cocktail. The Mai Tai gained popularity in the late 1950s and early 1960s and could be found in almost any establishment at least part way through.

Drink Recipe

40 ml of golden rum
10 ml grand marnier
20 ml lime juice
10 ml of orchard syrup

VOODO

It sounds corny, but don't be afraid to try it. This cocktail was created by Alex Kammerlin in 2002 in London, and the taste is deep and really well balanced. The rich flavor of the dark rum blends perfectly with the apple and lime juice, which add some acidity to the drink. Add a touch of sweetness with sweet vermouth and sugar syrup and the Voodoo is ready.

Preparation Method

Fill a shaker with ice. Add all the ingredients. Stir the ingredients thoroughly and pour into a chilled glass. Garnish the cocktail with grated cinnamon. You have just created a Voodoo!

Drink Recipe

40 ml of dark rum
20 ml sweet vermouth
80 ml apple juice
20 ml lime juice
20 ml sugar syrup

ZOMBIE

The first Zombie was created in 1934, and since then there have been more and more of them all over the globe. Such a mixture of different kinds of alcohol is certainly delicious, but in large quantities? - if you drink too much of it, you wake up in the morning as a zombie!

Preparation Method

Start by preparing a shaker. Fill it with ice, then measure the exact amounts of ingredients and pour them into the shaker. Shake vigorously and pour into a tall glass. Use a pineapple scooped over the edge of the glass as a garnish.

Drink Recipe

40 ml light rum
40 ml of golden rum
40 ml dark rum
10 ml of grand marnier
10 ml apricot liqueur
40 ml of orange juice
40 ml pineapple juice
20 ml lime juice
10 ml grenadine

DOLCE HAVANA

A sunny drink for all seasons.Feel like you're in Cuba in the middle of the season!

Preparation Method

Shake all ingredients in a shaker with ice and strain into a low glass filled with fresh ice. Use orange peel as garnish.

Drink Recipe

40 ml of pale rum
20 ml campari
20 ml of cointreau
40 ml of orange juice
40 ml of lime juice
10 ml sugar syrup

BLACK DIAMOND

Black Diamond is a tasty martini in a slightly dessert climate. The combination of hot espresso with rum and chocolate is incredibly aromatic and stimulating. The cocktail is on the one hand simple, and on the other rich and perfectly balanced.

Preparation Method

In the cocktail we need hot espresso, so start by brewing the coffee. Then add it to a shaker along with the cocoa liqueur and rum. Add ice and shake vigorously. Using a strainer, strain the cocktail into a chilled cocktail glass and sprinkle with grated white chocolate. Enjoy!

Drink Recipe

pale rum 40 ml
Cocoa liqueur 40 ml
Espresso - 40ml

EL PRESIDENTE

There are many versions of this cocktail. But the one using white rum, dry vermouth, cointreau, grenadine and angostura is the most popular and has become a Cuban classic. No wonder, because the El Presidente has the perfect balance of flavor and aroma, and it's perfect at any time of day or year.

Preparation Method

Pour the proper amounts of ingredients into a shaker filled with ice. Shake the ingredients and, using a bartender's strainer, strain into a chilled glass (without ice). Garnish the cocktail with orange peel. Done!

Drink Recipe

40 ml White rum
20 ml dry vermouth
5 ml cointreau
5 ml grenadine
angostura bitter - 2 dashes

RUM SOUR

Among the representatives of the Sour family, of course, could not miss a rum cocktail. It is smooth, sour, refreshing and perfectly balanced. Rum Sour is a cocktail that tastes good anytime, anywhere

Preparation Method

Shake all ingredients with ice in a shaker and strain into a low glass filled with ice using a strainer. For a better texture you can make a Dry Shake, i.e. after the first shake with ice do another shake without ice. Use orange peel for decoration.

Drink Recipe

40 ml Rum
20 ml Orange juice
20 ml Lime juice
10 ml Sugar syrup
10 ml Pasteurized protein

Audrey Saunders has made even a Mojito luxurious. All thanks to champagne, which he added to the popular mix. Add a cuppa glass instead of a glass and one of the most frequently ordered drinks becomes a sophisticated cocktail that no lady would be ashamed of.

Preparation Method

Add mint and remaining ingredients except champagne to a shaker with ice. Shake vigorously and strain into a chilled glass using a bar strainer. Top up with champagne and garnish with a mint leaf. Enjoy!

Drink Recipe

30 ml Aged rum
15 ml Lime juice
10 ml Sugar syrup
15 ml Champagne
Angostura - 2 dashes
Mint leaf x 6

CARIBBEAN PUNCH

Have you ever seen a movie where a really good party was held without a really good punchline? Neither have we! And if you want to throw one yourself, we definitely recommend the Caribbean Punch. As for the cocktail itself, it is probably the most tropical and holiday version of punch. And what can we say about the ingredients? As it is in a punch - a lot of different things.

Preparation Method

Pour all ingredients one at a time into a shaker filled with ice. Shake everything up in a shaker, then strain into a low glass filled with ice. Garnish your drink with a cocktail cherry and a pineapple chunk.

Drink Recipe

40 ml of golden rum
20 ml galliano
20 ml of malibu
20 ml almond liqueur
80 ml pineapple juice
30 ml lime juice
10 ml of grenadine

Despite appearances, the cocktail was not created in Hawaii, but comes straight from LA. The flavor, however, is one we might associate with those hot islands. It is sweet, fruity and somewhat tropical. Especially recommended for rum lovers.

Preparation Method

The cocktail is served in a chilled glass, so start by filling the glass with ice or putting it in the freezer for a few minutes, then prepare the shaker and all the ingredients. Pour all ingredients into the ice-filled shaker and shake vigorously. Using a bar strainer, strain the drink into a chilled glass (without ice). Garnish with a cocktail cherry and pineapple.

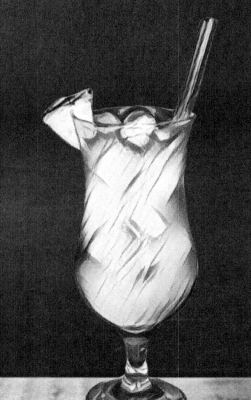

Drink Recipe

20 ml of pale rum
20 ml Southern Comfort
10 ml almond liqueur
20 ml of orange juice
20 ml pineapple juice

BAHAMA MAMA

The name and appearance give away a lot. Bahama Mama is a very exotic cocktail. A very aromatic combination of fruit with rum and malibu. A tasty, sun-drenched proposition for those craving a vacation.

Preparation Method

Prepare a tall cocktail glass. Chill the glass itself in the freezer or fill with ice. Pour all the ingredients for the drink into a shaker. Shake the ingredients with ice. Pour into a glass while draining the shaker. Garnish with a cocktail cherry and pineapple.

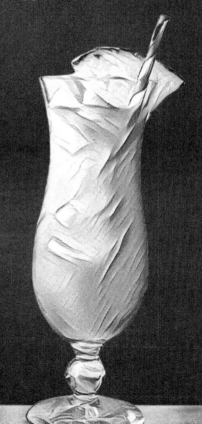

Drink Recipe

20 ml golden rum
20 ml dark rum
20 ml malibu
80 ml orange juice
80 ml pineapple juice
angostura bitter - 3 dashes

JAMAICAN SUNSET

The best words to describe the Jamaican sunset are: simple, nice and enjoyable. This cocktail is a tasty combination of dark rum, orange juice and cranberry juice.

Preparation Method

Jamaican Sunset is simple not only in composition but in execution! Compose it directly in a tall glass. Fill the glass with ice, then add rum, orange juice and cranberry juice one by one. Stir gently. You can garnish the cocktail with a slice of lime.

Drink Recipe

40 ml dark rum
80 ml orange juice
60 ml cranberry juice

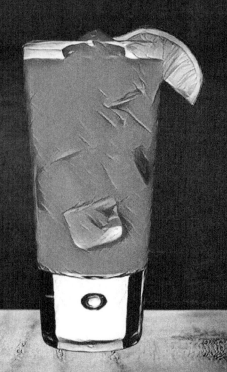

SHARK BITE

Shark Bite belongs rather to the group of sweet drinks, but by adding orange juice and lime juice it keeps the balance of flavors and will suit the tastes of almost every amateur. Why then the name of the cocktail? The answer is simple - in some versions of the drink our glass looks like the blue surface of the ocean, in which a red drop of blood was spilled. One thing can be said about Shark Bite - it is very impressive in appearance and excellent in taste.

Preparation Method

Pour dark rum, cointreau, orange juice and lime juice into a blender. Then add a few ice cubes and mix thoroughly. Pour the cocktail into a tall glass filled with ice. Finally, splash some grenadine on top and garnish with a piece of pineapple. If you want to get the effect of blue ocean surface and drops of blood, add an additional 30 ml of Blue Curacao before pouring the grenadine and stir the drink.

Drink Recipe

60 ml of dark rum
20 ml cointreau
60 ml of orange juice
20 ml lime juice
20 ml of grenadine

PAINKILLER

The Painkiller is one of the popular tiki cocktails of the mid-20th century. Its history dates back to the Soggy Dollar bar of the British Virgin Islands. In practice, it is a richly flavored and fruity rum-based cocktail.

Preparation Method

Start preparing the cocktail by chilling a tall glass. Put some ice cubes in it or put it in the freezer for a few minutes. Then pour all the ingredients into a shaker and top up with ice. Shake for about 10 seconds. Pour the cocktail into a chilled glass and garnish with a piece of pineapple.

Drink Recipe

60 ml dark rum
20 ml orange juice
80 ml Pineapple juice
20 ml Coconut cream

PEDRO COLLINS

This delicious and simple lemonade with rum in the background is perfect for those who can't decide if their favorite cocktail is a Tom Collins or a Daiquiri. The Pedro Collins is a blend perfectly in the middle. Rum, bubbles, lime, lemon and sugar syrup... sound interesting? Be sure to give it a try.

Preparation Method

Pour all ingredients (except sparkling water!) into a shaker and shake vigorously for about 10-15 seconds. Pour the whole thing into a tall school filled with fresh ice, then top off with sparkling water. The final step to the perfect cocktail is garnish! Use a lime wedge as a garnish... and you're done! Enjoy!

Drink Recipe

40 ml white rum
100 ml Sparkling water
10 ml ime juice
10 ml lemon juice
20 ml sugar syrup

MONKEY WRENCH

A cocktail for followers of the "less is more" principle. Simple, but very pleasant and tasty. Monkey Wrench is a combination of dark rum and grapefruit juice. Drinking this simple cocktail you will find that rum will always go well in fruit drink recipes.

Preparation Method

Monkey Wrench should be composed directly in the glass. Put a few ice cubes in a tall glass. Then pour in the appropriate amounts of ingredients.

Drink Recipe

60 ml - dark rum
120 ml of grapefruit juice

ESPRESSO MARTINI

Espresso Martini is a strong drink, whose greatest advantage is to awaken - not only the taste buds. Its composition (as you can easily guess) includes espresso. The author of the original recipe is Dick Bradsell, who first served it in the eighties at the Freds Club in London, at the request of a client who needed something to wake her up.

Preparation Method

Mix ingredients in a shaker filled with ice. Shake the shaker vigorously. Pour the mixture into a martini glass. Serve without ice.

Drink Recipe

60 ml vanilla rum
55 ml of coffee liqueur
45 ml of chilled coffee

TEQUILA SUNRSIE

Tequila Sunrise was created in Agua Caliente, a resort (literally) located in Tijuana, Mexico, where alcohol-thirsty Americans vacationed during Prohibition.

Preparation Method

A portion of good tequila is mixed, in a tall glass filled with ice, with orange juice, and grenadine syrup is poured lightly on top.

Drink Recipe

60 ml silver tequila
120 ml orange juice
10 ml grenadine syrup

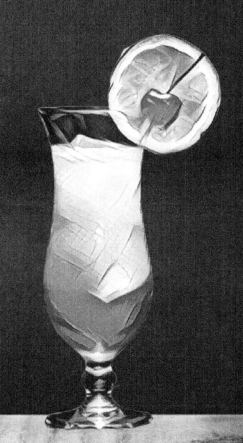

MARGARITA

Very popular to order at the pub, especially in summer. The sweet and sour mix is the most preferred by us mammals.On the one hand it is refreshing and on the other hand it is energetic.

Preparation Method

First prepare the glass: rub the rim of the glass with a lime wedge, then gently "dip" the outside of the rim of the glass in salt. This will create a fantastic contrast to the sweet and sour margarita. Next, shake the ingredients in a shaker and strain without ice into a chilled glass.

Drink Recipe

30 ml silver tequila
30 ml cointreau
15 ml of lime juice
15 ml of lemon juice
15 ml of sugar syrup

TEQUILA SOUR

Satisfying if you run out of ingredients for a "Margarita," but is that the only time? Tequila Sour is a distinct, sweet and sour cocktail that is sure to be suitable for any occasion. It also comes in a version with the addition of chicken protein. Simply add the white of one egg to the ingredients in a shaker and shake vigorously.

Preparation Method

Start by properly preparing the glass in which you will serve the cocktail. Fill it with ice and set it aside for some time or put it in the freezer for a few minutes. Then, pour all the ingredients into a shaker with ice and mix thoroughly. Using a bar strainer, strain the drink into a chilled glass. Use a quarter of a lemon impaled on the rim of the glass and a cocktail cherry as garnish.

Drink Recipe

60 ml silver tequila
10 ml of lime juice
10 ml of lemon juice
20 ml of sugar syrup

EL DIABLO

We present a fantastic cocktail for thirsty tequila fans. With the addition of currant liqueur, Ginger ale and lime and lemon juice, El Diablo is not only very tasty but also very refreshing. If you like ginger, this will be your summer favorite.

Preparation Method

Use a tall glass to serve the cocktail. To chill the glass, fill it with ice and set it aside for a few minutes or place it in the freezer while you prepare the cocktail. Pour appropriate amounts of tequila, currant liqueur, lime juice, lemon juice and sugar syrup into a shaker filled with ice. Shake the ingredients and pour into a tall glass. Finally, pour in the Ginger ale. Use the lime wedges as a garnish.

Drink Recipe

40 ml silver tequila
20 ml currant liqueur
20 ml of lime juice
10 ml of lemon juice
10 ml sugar syrup
100 ml Ginger Ale

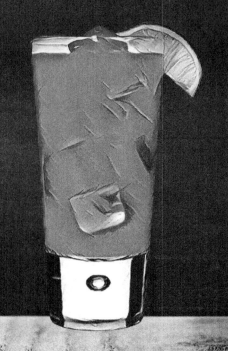

VAMPIRO

Not as scary as the name suggests. Vampiro is a sweeter version of Bloody Mary with Mexican flair. It is an interesting alternative for those who are not impressed by the well-known combination of vodka and tomato juice. The addition of grenadine makes the cocktail much more drinkable.

Preparation Method

Shake all ingredients with ice in a shaker and strain without ice into a low glass filled with ice. Use lime quarters to garnish.

Drink Recipe

40 ml tequila
20 ml orange juice
20 ml tomato juice
10 ml lime juice
10 ml grenadine
5 drops TABASCO® Sauce
1 pinch of salt
1 pinch of pepper

MATADOR

A cocktail that every "Margarita" fan will love. What makes it different is that it is bolder and more fruity. Simple and quick to make, but with the perfect balance of flavor, it is one of the most refreshing drinks. Most importantly, it goes perfectly with grilled dishes and spicy and salty snacks. In conclusion, the Matador is the perfect drink for summer for all tequila lovers.

Preparation Method

Use a tall glass to serve the cocktail. In a shaker filled with ice, pour the right amounts of tequila, orange liqueur, lime juice and pineapple juice. Shake the ingredients and pour into a tall glass. Use pineapple segments or orange peel as a garnish.

Drink Recipe

40 ml of tequila reposado
20 ml orange liqueur
10 ml lime juice
20 ml pineapple juice

Iguana is an interesting combination of
vodka. We advise you to be really careful wit...

...ced with
head.

Preparation Method

Prepare an ice shaker and pour equal amounts of all ingredients into it. Using a bar strainer, strain the prepared drink (without ice) into a chilled vodka glass.

Drink Recipe

15 ml vodka
15 ml silver tequila
15 ml coffee liqueur

AYAN

...ffee and pineapple. Take my word for it, Mayan is a cocktail with a ...g combination of flavors. It is not only well balanced, but also very ...e for yourself!

Preparation Method

This cocktail should be composed directly in a low glass. Fill it with ice cubes and then pour in all the ingredients. Gently stir the cocktail. Ready!

Drink Recipe

40 ml silver tequila
10 ml coffee liqueur
60 ml pineapple juice

PLAYA DEL MAR

Playa Del Mar is one of many proposals for fans of fruity Margaritas. This time it's cranberry and pineapple, a not-so-typical combination that makes this cocktail perfect for both summer and autumn.

Preparation Method

Start by chilling the glass in which you will serve the cocktail - fill it with ice and set aside while you prepare the cocktail or put it in the freezer for a few minutes. Then prepare a shaker and pour the ice into it. Shake vigorously and strain without ice into a chilled glass. Garnish the cocktail with a pineapple wedge. Enjoy!

Drink Recipe

20 ml silver tequila
10 ml cointreau
20 ml cranberry juice
20 ml pineapple juice
10 ml lime juice
10 ml sugar syrup

GOLDEN DRAGON

The Golden Dragon is an extremely fragrant tequila-based cocktail. As usual, the combination of Mexican vodka and fruit comes out great. The aromas of green bananas, passion fruit, apple and lime make this drink very exotic.

Preparation Method

Start by preparing the glass in which you will serve the cocktail. To chill it, put it in the freezer for a few minutes or fill it with ice and set it aside while you prepare the drink. Put some ice in a shaker and then, using a jigger, carefully measure and pour all the ingredients. Shake vigorously and pour the cocktail into a chilled glass. Garnish with a piece of apple.

Drink Recipe

40 ml tequila reposado
20 ml green banana liqueur
20 ml passion fruit syrup
40 ml apple juice
20 ml lime juice

ULTIMA PALABRA

Ultima Palabra means "last word" in Spanish. This explains a lot when it turns out that this cocktail is a variation on the classic "Last Word". Instead of using gin, we base the drink on Mexican vodka, and add a touch of lavender syrup to give it a twist. The result is a well-balanced cocktail. Our final word is simply delicious!

Preparation Method

Start by filling a glass with ice or putting it in the freezer for a few minutes. Pour all ingredients into a shaker filled with ice and shake vigorously. Strain (without ice) the drink thus prepared into a chilled glass.

Drink Recipe

30 ml tequila reposado
20 ml Green Chartreuse
15 ml maraschino
5 ml lavender syrup
20 ml lime juice

MEXICO CITY

Mexico City is nothing less than another successful version of the Margarita. A fruity combination on a Mexican vodka can't go wrong. Grand Marnier, cranberry juice and lime create a refreshing taste and aroma, so this cocktail is perfect for warm afternoons.

Preparation Method

Start by preparing the glass in which you will serve the cocktail. To chill it, put it in the freezer for a few minutes or fill it with ice and set it aside while you prepare the drink. Put ice in a shaker and then pour all the ingredients into it. Shake vigorously in a shaker and strain into a chilled cocktail glass (without ice) using a strainer. Garnish with a lime wedge. Done!

Drink Recipe

40 ml silver tequila
20 ml grand marnier
10 ml cranberry juice
10 ml lime juice
10 ml sugar syrup

EL TORADO

El Torado is a cocktail for lovers of simplicity and elegance. The combination of tequila, vermouth and apple juice is dry yet refined and fruity. It is one of the most popular Mexican cocktails, of course it can't beat a Margarita, but it is very popular and often ordered by Mexican citizens.

Preparation Method

Start by preparing the glass in which you will serve the cocktail. To chill it, put it in the freezer for a few minutes or fill it with ice and set it aside while you prepare the drink. Put ice in a shaker and then pour all the ingredients into it. Shake the shaker vigorously and, using a strainer, strain into a chilled cocktail glass (without ice). Garnish with a slice of apple. Done!

Drink Recipe

60 ml tequila reposado
20 ml dry vermouth
40 ml apple juice

ADIOS

Are you having a Mexican style house party? You can't miss this shot. Even more so if you have people watching their weight among your guests. Adios is a simple in composition and execution low-calorie shot. It is composed only of silver tequila and coffee liqueur. Be sure to try it!

Preparation Method

Pour a few ice cubes into a shaker, then pour in both ingredients. Shake vigorously (for about 10-15 seconds). Adiós!

Drink Recipe

15 ml silver tequila
15 ml coffee liqueur

CACTUS JACK

Cactus Jack seduces at first sight with its beautiful green color. We can say about our cocktail that it is a pineapple relative of the famous Margarita, and its perfectly balanced taste captured the heart and palate of many an alcoholic!

Preparation Method

Fill the glass with ice and set aside for a few minutes to chill or place in the freezer while you prepare the cocktail. Put ice in a shaker and then measure and pour exact amounts of cocktail ingredients. Shake vigorously for about 10-15 seconds and strain (without ice) into a chilled cocktail glass. Use pineapple as a garnish.

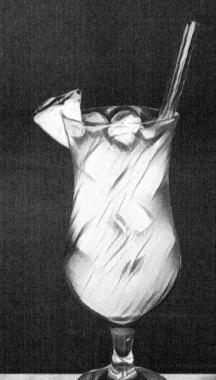

Drink Recipe

20 ml silver tequila
20 ml blue curacao
20 ml orange juice
20 ml pineapple juice
10 ml lemon juice

CHIHUAHUA MARGARITA

Chihuahua is a simple in composition, but rich in flavor Margarita. We compose it, of course, on a base of tequila. The second and almost final component is grapefruit juice. The addition of bitters is necessary to spice up the cocktail. I must admit that this is a great proposal for lovers of the Mexican drink.

Preparation Method

Put the cocktail glass in the freezer for a few minutes or fill it with ice and set aside to chill. Put ice in a shaker, pour in the right amount of ingredients and shake vigorously. Strain the cocktail into a chilled glass (no ice). Done! Enjoy!

Drink Recipe

60 ml tequila reposado
60 ml grapefruit juice
10 ml agave syrup
angostura bitter - 3 dash

LOVED UP

The Loved Up is a raspberry Margarita under the lid. The recipe for this delicious cocktail dates back to 2002, when it was first served at the Merc Bar in New York City. It is a fantastic fruity option for tequila fans.

Preparation Method

Start by preparing the glass in which you will serve the cocktail. To chill it, put it in the freezer for a few minutes or fill it with ice and set it aside while you prepare the drink. Put ice in a shaker and then pour all the ingredients into it. Shake vigorously in a shaker and strain into a chilled cocktail glass (without ice) using a strainer. Garnish with raspberries.

Drink Recipe

40 ml silver tequila
20 ml chambord
10 ml Coinreau triple sec
10 ml lime juice
10 ml lemon juice
10 ml sugar syrup

RED HOOKER

Specific in taste, red drink based on tequila. It is quite bold, it lacks balance of flavors, but it can find its fans. Especially recommended for all fans of fruity flavors and tequila. Just try it!

Preparation Method

The first step in our recipe will be to prepare the glass in which you will serve the drink. Fill it with ice and let it chill for a few minutes or place it in the freezer while you prepare the cocktail. Put ice in a shaker and then, using a jigger, measure and pour the exact amounts of the cocktail ingredients. Shake vigorously for about 10-15 seconds and strain (without ice) into a chilled cocktail glass. Use a slice of peach as a garnish.

Drink Recipe

40 ml silver tequila
20 ml Chambord liqueur
10 ml lemon juice

JALISCO FLOWER

Jalisco Flower is a true pleasure. A wonderful fruity aroma, subtle taste and a delicate bubbly finish. This fantastic cocktail was composed in 2008 by Vincenzo Marianella. If you love sparkling cocktails, this is a must try. I guarantee that it will become your favorite!

Preparation Method

To prepare this cocktail we need a tall glass. To chill, we put a few ice cubes in it and set it aside. Meanwhile, pour the right amounts of tequila, liqueur and juice into a shaker. Fill the shaker with ice and shake for about 10-15 seconds. Strain the contents of the shaker (without ice) into a chilled glass, top up with champagne and stir gently. The garnish is left - we use grapefruit zest to decorate.

Drink Recipe

20 ml tequila reposado
30 ml elderflower liqueur
40 ml grapefruit juice
80 ml champagne

CHIMAYO

The Chimayo is a great option for those looking for a cocktail that is simple in construction but complex in flavor. Tequila, currant, lemon and apple are an interesting, refreshing and fresh combination.

Preparation Method

Start by preparing the glass in which you will serve the cocktail. To chill it, put it in the freezer for a few minutes or fill it with ice and set it aside while you prepare the drink. Put ice in a shaker and then pour all the ingredients into it. Shake vigorously and strain into a chilled cocktail glass (without ice) using a strainer.

Drink Recipe

40 ml tequila reposado
20 ml currant liqueur
40 ml apple juice
10 ml lemon juice

FLORIDITA MARGARITA

This fruity Margarita is perfect for any occasion. It is not only very aromatic, but also very well balanced in terms of taste, and its appearance is very inviting. It is not only a real treat for tequila lovers, but also a perfect time killer for anyone who tries it.

Preparation Method

Pour the proper amounts of ingredients into a shaker filled with ice. Shake the ingredients and, using a bartender's strainer, strain into a pre-chilled glass (without ice). Done!

Drink Recipe

40 ml tequila reposado
20 ml Cointreau triple sec
20 ml cranberry juice
40 ml grapefruit juice
20 ml lime juice
20 ml sugar syrup

MEXICAN MULE

As the name suggests, this is a refreshing classic with a Mexican twist. It is not only very tasty but also spiked with tequila. Mexican Mule is definitely a cocktail for hot days!

Preparation Method

Fill a shaker with ice, pour tequila, lime juice and sugar syrup and shake vigorously. Pour into a tall glass and top off with ginger ale. The final step to the perfect cocktail is the garnish! Garnish your drink with a quarter of a lime.

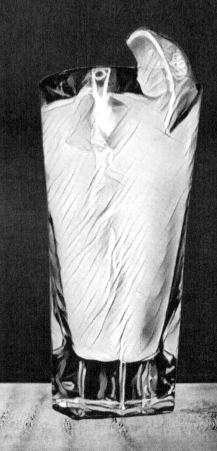

Drink Recipe

40 ml silver tequila
100 ml ginger ale
120 ml ime juice
10 ml sugar syrup

AMIGO SHOT

Party in Mexican style? Amigo Shot comes to the rescue! This tasty tequila-based cocktail will not only fit the mood of your house party, but also stimulate your guests to have fun. Just remember, don't overdo it

Preparation Method

Serve in a shot glass. Note: Order matters here. Gently arrange the layers in the following order: coffee liqueur, silver tequila, cream. This Mexican mix is sure to please your guests! Enjoy.

Drink Recipe

15 ml silver tequila
15 ml coffee liqueur
15 ml cream

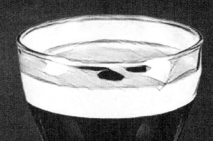

JAPANESE SLIPPER

Japanese slipper is an easily memorable drink with a unique color. Silver tequila, melon liqueur and lime juice make a very interesting aromatic combination. Sweetness of liqueur and sugar syrup perfectly contrasts with citrus taste of lime. Simple, quick to make and very enjoyable.

Preparation Method

Start by preparing the glass in which you will serve the cocktail. To chill it, put it in the freezer for a few minutes or fill it with ice and set it aside while you prepare the drink. Put ice in a shaker and then pour all the ingredients into it. Shake vigorously in a shaker and strain into a chilled cocktail glass (without ice) using a strainer.

Drink Recipe

40 ml silver tequila
40 ml melon liqueur
10 ml of lime juice
10 ml of sugar syrup

MEXICANO

This time something to warm you up. Tequila cocktails are not only fruit Margaritas, we can also use Mexican vodka to create the perfect drink for chilly afternoons. Mexicano will be perfect for such days, especially if you need a little boost. This cocktail is simply coffee with electricity!

Preparation Method

Pour hot water into a glass with ears, then once the glass is warm, empty it and start making the cocktail. Pour the tequila, liqueur, and then the hot coffee on the bottom in order. Gently place a layer of cream on top of the cocktail.

Drink Recipe

30 ml tequila reposado
15 ml Grand Marnier
80 ml lack coffee
cream - 1 spoon

TOM COLLINS

This is one of the most popular cocktails made with a gin base. Besides juniper, this drink also contains lemon juice, sugar and sparkling water. The recipe for Tom Collins was published in the United States quite a long time ago, back in 1876.

Preparation Method

This drink doesn't require much skill on your part. It only takes 5 minutes to turn gin, sugar syrup, lime juice and sparkling water into a classic drink. Put gin, sugar syrup and lime juice in a shaker filled with ice. Shake and pour into a tall glass, then top up with sparkling water and you're ready to go!

Drink Recipe

60 ml gin
10 ml lemon juice
10 ml lime juice
20 ml sugar syrup
80 ml sparkling water

GIN & TONIC

Gin & Tonic is one of Britain's favorite drinks, plus it's very simple to make because it only has four ingredients - gin, tonic, ice and garnish. However, even such a simple recipe requires some skill in preparation.

Preparation Method

Pour a few ice cubes into a tall glass, then pour in the gin and tonic. Use a quarter lime as a garnish.

Drink Recipe

40 ml gin
80 ml tonic

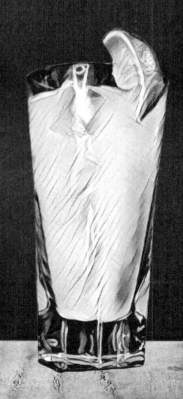

GIMLET

Uncomplicated, but very tasty. The Gimlet cocktail has been on bartenders' charts since 1928, and the first description depicted it as a drink made of gin with a little lime and bubbles.

Preparation Method

Put ice in a shaker, pour in the right amount of ingredients and shake vigorously. Using a bar strainer, strain the cocktail into a low glass filled with fresh ice. Garnish the cocktail with a quarter lime.

Drink Recipe

60 ml gin
10 ml lime juice
10 ml sugar syrup

MARTINI

The origin of the Martini is very unclear and we will probably never know where it got its name. Paradoxically, the simplest cocktails, consisting of only two or three ingredients, are the easiest to spoil. In other words, minimalism makes such a drink is very transparent, and therefore any imperfections can be seen clearly. Martini is such a drink in which the exact amount of ingredients poured and their temperature is of great importance.

Preparation Method

Blend all ingredients in a shaker with ice and strain into a chilled glass. Use a green olive as a garnish.

Drink Recipe

60 ml gin
10 ml dry vermouth

FRENCH 75

French 75 has been known and loved by all spirits lovers since 1920, when its recipe was first published. Watch out, because this intriguing combination of gin and champagne really goes to your head!

Preparation Method

Start by preparing the glass in which you will serve the drink. Fill it with ice and set aside to chill or put in the freezer while you prepare the cocktail. Pour the gin, lemon juice and sugar syrup into a shaker. Shake all the ingredients in a shaker and pour the cocktail into the prepared glass and top up with champagne or sparkling wine. Use a cocktail cherry to garnish. Enjoy!

Drink Recipe

40 ml of gin
80 ml champagne or sparkling wine
20 ml lemon juice
20 ml sugar syrup

NEGRONI

Negroni is a drink that is currently breaking records of popularity. It is the most popular drink recommended by bartenders and the second most popular drink ordered by bar guests. The history of Negroni dates back to the beginning of the 20th century and it is said that this drink was an evolution of the popular in Italy Americano.

Preparation Method

Mix all ingredients with ice in a bar shaker, then strain into a low glass filled with ice. Use lemon zest for garnish.

Drink Recipe

30 ml gin
30 ml Lillet Blanc
30 ml Suze

GIBSON

What do Sandra Bullock and a drink called Gibson have in common? The answer lies in The Net, a 1995 movie, Gibson was the favorite drink of the character played by Sandra.

Preparation Method

Start by preparing the glass in which you will serve the cocktail. To chill, put it in the freezer for a few minutes or fill with ice and set aside while you prepare the drink. Pour gin and dry vermouth into a shaker filled with ice. Stir the ingredients thoroughly and strain into a chilled glass. Garnish the cocktail with cocktail onions.

Drink Recipe

60 ml gin
10 ml dry vermouth

BASIL SMASH

Basil Smash is another proposal of a refreshing cocktail based on gin. This drink was developed by Jorg Meyer in Le Lion cocktail bar in Hamburg in 2008. It is characterized by lightness, green color and simplicity! It is an ideal proposition for the coming summer.

Preparation Method

In the bottom of a shaker, gently mash the basil with the gin, then add the other two ingredients. Shake everything with ice cubes and strain into an ice-filled lowball glass. Garnish with basil leaves.

Drink Recipe

40 ml Gin
20 ml fresh lemon juice
10 ml sugar syrup
10 basil leaves

GIN SOUR

Another representative of the "sour" family, whose base is gin. It is certainly an interesting proposition for those who hate whisky, but like simple cocktails. You can omit the protein and angostura from the recipe, but they give the right consistency and turn up the aroma of the cocktail.

Preparation Method

In order to properly whip up the protein, you need to shake the cocktail very hard. For this purpose, when making a Gin sour, it is worth using a preparation technique called "dry shake". This method involves shaking all the ingredients without ice and then shaking again with ice. This method produces a very nice looking shake, with a thick foam on the surface. An additional advantage of using protein is that the drink changes its texture, becoming silkier on the tongue. Shake all ingredients without ice and then again with ice. Pour into a low glass and use orange peel to garnish.

Drink Recipe

40 ml Gin
20 ml Lemon juice
10 ml Sugar syrup
Pasteurized protein
Angostura - 3 dashe

ORANGE BLOOSOM

A delicious and delicate cocktail with a distinct citrus flavour. Especially recommended for gin fans. Are you looking for a drink idea that will impress your friends and at the same time is very simple to make? With help comes Orange bossom.

Preparation Method

Start by preparing a low glass in which to serve the drink. Fill it with ice and set aside to cool or place in the freezer while you prepare the cocktail. Pour ice into a shaker, then pour in the ingredients and shake vigorously. Pour the drink into a chilled cocktail glass. Use orange peel to garnish. Good luck!

Drink Recipe

40 ml gin
20 ml Cointreau
40 ml orange juice
20 ml lime juice
5 ml Grenadine

CASINO

If you are a fan of the tart and bitter taste of gin and like compositions that are heavier, then we have the perfect suggestion for you. Cocktail Casino!

Preparation Method

Put a few ice cubes in a shaker, then pour in all the ingredients and shake. Pour into a chilled glass. Use a maraschino cherry to garnish.

Drink Recipe

60 ml gin
30 ml Luxardo Maraschino Liqueur
20 ml lemon juice
1 dash Orange Bitter

JASMINE

Jasmine is a pleasant and aromatic cocktail with citrus flavors. It was created in the 1990s in California and was created by Paul Harrington. Fans of Campari will love it.

Preparation Method

Prepare a glass and put a few ice cubes in it to chill. Pour all ingredients into a shaker with ice and shake. Strain the cocktail through a bar strainer into a chilled glass (without ice). Garnish with lemon zest. Good luck!

Drink Recipe

20 ml gin
10 ml Campari
10 ml Cointreau
20 ml lemon juice
10 ml sugar syrup

JACUZZI

This cocktail is just perfect for a Jacuzzi party. From the amount of bubbles you will go crazy! The drink itself is easily digestible, but also dangerous. Be careful, because the gin, champagne and peach liqueur will quickly turn your head!

Preparation Method

Compose the Jacuzzi directly in a champagne glass. Add the gin, peach liqueur and orange juice one by one. Finally pour the champagne. Use a slice of peach as a garnish.

Drink Recipe

20 ml gin
40 ml peach liqueur
40 ml orange juice
60 ml champagne

BIKINI MARTINI

This blue martini is the result of mixing gin, blue curacao, peach liqueur, and lemon juice. The taste of the cocktail is as appropriate to the name, and with its distinct color, it will be great for pool parties.

Preparation Method

Start by preparing the glass in which you will serve your cocktail. Fill it with ice and set aside for a few minutes. Put the ice in a shaker, then pour in all the ingredients one by one and shake. Using a bar strainer, strain the cocktail from the shaker or jar (without ice) into a chilled glass. The last thing you need to do is garnish the cocktail - add a lemon zest to the top of the cocktail and... done!

Drink Recipe

40 ml gin
20 ml blue curacao
10 ml peach liqueur
10 ml lemon juice

LONDON CALLING

We know for a fact that the London Calling cocktail was first served in 2003 at the Oxo Tower Bar & Brasserie in London. We also know that since its inception, the London Calling cocktail has enjoyed great popularity, and its classic taste accompanies banquets around the world!

Preparation Method

Start by preparing the glass in which you will serve the cocktail. Fill it with ice and set aside for some time or put in the freezer for a few minutes to chill. Pour the carefully measured ingredients into a bar shaker filled with ice and stir vigorously. Using a bar strainer, strain the cocktail into a chilled glass (without ice). Use orange peel as garnish. Enjoy!

Drink Recipe

40 ml gin
10 ml sweet vermouth
30 ml tartar liqueur
2 dashes of orange bitters

CLOVER CLUB

Clover Club is a drink delicate in taste, full of the aroma of fresh raspberries. Ideal for gin fans who are looking for light, pleasant solutions.

Preparation Method

Start by freezing the glass in which you will serve the cocktail. To do this, put it in the freezer for a while or fill it with ice. Crush raspberries (half) in the bottom of a cocktail glass. Add lemon juice, gin and the white of one egg. Shake in a shaker for about 15 seconds, add ice and shake again. Strain the cocktail through a strainer into a glass of your choice. Decorate with raspberries. Done!

Drink Recipe

Egg white from 1 piece
20 ml lemon juice
60 ml Gin
Raspberries - 10 pieces
20 ml Dry white vermouth

WHAT THE HELL

Gin, vermouth, apricot liqueur, lime juice and sugar syrup... What the Hell? No, that's not a mistake in the recipe. Trust us, What the Hell is a sensational combination of flavors!

Preparation Method

The first step is to chill the glass in which you will serve the cocktail - fill it with ice or put it in the freezer for a few minutes. Put some ice in a shaker, then pour in all the ingredients one by one and shake. Using a bar strainer, strain the cocktail from the shaker into the chilled glass. The last thing you need to do is garnish the cocktail with orange peel... and you're done! Enjoy.

Drink Recipe

40 ml gin
20 ml dry vermouth
20 ml apricot liqueur
10 ml lime juice
10 ml sugar syrup

OLD FRIEND

Bittersweet, dry and tart flavors all in one glass and very well balanced. Old Friend is a close friend of Negroni, which will be perfect as an aperitif at a dinner with old friends.

Preparation Method

Put ice in a shaker, pour in the right amount of ingredients and shake vigorously. Using a bar strainer, strain the cocktail into a chilled cocktail glass and garnish with a garnish of grapefruit seed.

Drink Recipe

60 ml gin
30 ml grapefruit juice
20 ml Campari
10 ml elderflower liqueur

INK MARTINI

A drink that resembles ink in color? In front of you bows the Ink Martini, which was created by Gentian Naci. The recipe for this drink was created in 2002 in England, and its components are gin, Blue Curacao, peach liqueur and cranberry juice. Simple and tasty!

Preparation Method

Before you move on to making the cocktail, prepare the glass in which you will serve your cocktail. Fill it with ice and set it aside for a few minutes or place it in the freezer while you prepare your drink. Mix all ingredients in a shaker with ice and strain into a chilled glass. Now it's time for the final step, the garnish! The garnish for our cocktail will be orange peel.

Drink Recipe

20 ml gin
10 ml Blue Curacao liqueur
10 ml peach liqueur
40 ml cranberry juice

MILIONAIRE'S MARTINI

The Millionaire's Martini was created during Prohibition and we've been enjoying this sparkling, classic cocktail ever since. Adding champagne to the classic vermouth and gin combination is the perfect way to turn up the drink and show off your uniqueness. Plus it is actually very refined.

Preparation Method

Start by chilling the glass in which you will serve the cocktail - fill it with ice and set aside while you prepare the cocktail or put it in the freezer for a few minutes. Then prepare a shaker and pour ice into it, then pour equal amounts of gin and vermouth. Stir gently and, using a strainer, strain into a glass prepared beforehand (without ice). Top off your cocktail with champagne, Prosecco or Cava.

Drink Recipe

60 ml gin
60 ml dry vermouth
30 ml champagne

ANGEL'S DELIGHT

This cocktail is creamy like melted ice cream. Angel'sDelight is a great dessert cocktail to serve at a party. It tastes and looks heavenly. The grenadine gives a pink candy color that makes no shortage of takers for this drink. The name of the cocktail is right on point, it is a true delight.

Preparation Method

Start by preparing the glass in which you will serve the cocktail - fill it with ice to chill it and set aside for a few minutes or place it in the freezer while you prepare the cocktail. Put ice in a shaker and then pour the carefully measured ingredients. Shake vigorously for about 10-15 seconds and strain (without ice) into a chilled glass. Garnish the rim of the glass with a raspberry and... done!

Drink Recipe

20 ml gin
20 ml Cointreau
40 ml cream
10 ml grenadine

DNA

DNA is a very crisp and clear gin-based cocktail. The cocktail combines the sweetness of apricot liqueur, citrus acidity and intensity of gin, resulting in a great and perfectly balanced harmony of flavours.

Preparation Method

Put the cocktail glass in the freezer for a few minutes or fill it with ice and set aside to chill. Put ice in a shaker, pour in the right amount of ingredients and shake vigorously. Using a bar strainer, strain the cocktail into a chilled cocktail glass (without ice). Garnish the cocktail with orange zest.

Drink Recipe

40 ml gin
20 ml apricot liqueur
20 ml lemon juice
10 ml sugar syrup
3 dashes of orange bitters

NIGHTMARE MARTINI

The name of this cocktail is totally inappropriate. It has nothing to do with a nightmare. On the contrary, it is a very interesting proposition of a fruit martini. All you need to compose it is gin, dubonnet, cherry liqueur and orange juice. There is nothing to be afraid of!

Preparation Method

Pour the measured ingredients into a shaker. Shake vigorously for about 10-15 seconds, then strain over ice into a chilled glass. Garnish with a cocktail cherry.

Drink Recipe

20 ml gin
20 ml Dubonnet Red
10 ml cherry liqueur
40 ml orange juice

GINA

This super summer cocktail is actually a currant version of the Tom Collins. If this classic drink is not fruity enough for you, you should definitely try its fruity version. Such a refreshing drink is perfect for hot summer days.

Preparation Method

Put ice in a shaker, then pour the gin, lemon juice, currant liqueur and sugar syrup and shake vigorously. Pour into a tall glass and top up with sparkling water. The last step to a perfect cocktail is the garnish! Forest fruits are perfect as garnish.

Drink Recipe

40 ml gin
20 ml currant liqueur
80 ml carbonated water
20 ml lemon juice
10 ml sugar syrup

THE LAST WORD

This pale green cocktail is a Prohibition-era item. The combination of gin, green chartreuse, maraschino and lime is elegant, aromatic and has a very good balance of sweetness, tartness and herbs. If these are your tastes, be sure to try it!

Preparation Method

Shake the ingredients in a shaker and strain without ice into a chilled cocktail glass - fill with ice to chill and let sit while you prepare the drink, or place in the freezer for a few minutes. Pour all ingredients into a shaker filled with ice and shake. Using a bar strainer, strain the drink into the chilled glass and garnish with a maraschino cherry. Enjoy!

Drink Recipe

40 ml Gin
30 ml Green Chartreuse
30 ml Maraschino
30 ml Lime juice

GRILL PARTY

CUBA LIBRE

CHIHUAHUA MARGARITA

BLOODY MARY

TENNESSEE ICED TEA

PEDRO COLLINS

MOJITO

CHRISTMAS

COSMOPOLITAN

RAFAELLO

EL PRESIDENTE

TENNESSEE FIRE BEER

BURBON COOKIE

ESPRESSO MARTINI

NEW YEAR'S EVE

VESPER MARTINI

OLD FASHIONED

MILIONAIRE'S MARTINI

FRENCH 75

JACUZZI

DOLCE HAVANA

GENTLEMEN'S NIGHT

WHISKEY SOUR

GODFATHER

IRISH BOULEVARDIER

MAI TAI

WHITE RUSSIAN

BASIL SMASH

LADIES PARTY

SCREAMING ORGASM

BIKINI MARTINI

SEX ON THE BEACH

TEQUILA SUNRISE

CAIPIRINHA

PORNSTAR MARTINI

INDEX

ACPULCO 65
ADAM&EVE 50
ADIOS 100
AGGRAVATION 46
ALGONQUIN 57
AMIGO SHOT 109
ANGEL'S DELIGHT 133
BAHAMA MAMA 79
BASIL SMASH 120
BIKINI MARTINI 126
BLACK DIAMOND 73
BLACK RUSSIAN 16
BLOODY MARRY 18
BRAINSTROM 58
BUCKET LIST 22
BURBON COOKIE 45
CACTUS JACK 101
CAIPIRINHA 62
CAIPIROSKA 15
CALIFORNIA LEMONADE 24
CARIBEEAN PUNCH 77
CASINO 123
CHICHUAUA MARGARITA 102
CHILLOUT MARTINI 28
CHIMAYO 106
CLOVER CLUB 128
COSMOPOLITAN 9
CUBA LIBRE 61
CUNNINGHAM MARTINI 52
DAIQUIRI 64
DIRTY DANCING 21
DNA 134
DOLCE HAVANA 72
EL DIABLO 90
EL PRESIDENTE 74
EL TORADO 99
ESPRESSO MARTINI 85
FLORIDITA MARGARITA 107
FLYING SCOTSMAN 56
FRENCH 75 117
GIBSON 119
GIMLET 115
GIN & TONIC 114
GIN SOUR 121

GINA 136
GODFATHER 37
GOLDEN DRAGON 96
HAND GRANADE 29
HAT THE HELL 129
HAWAIIAN 78
IGUANA 93
INK MARTINI 131
IRISH BOULEVARDIER 41
IRISH COFFE 47
JACUZZI 125
JAISCO FLOWER 105
JAMAICAN SUNSET 80
JAPANESSE SLIPPER 110
JASMINE 124
JUNGLE JUICE 66
KAMIKADZE SHOT 20
KENTUCKY COLONEL 44
KENTUCKY TEA 51
KILLER PUNCH 27
LONDON CALLING 127
LONG ISLAND ICE TEA 13
LOVED UP 103
LYNCHBURG LEMONADE 42
MADROSCA 30
MAI TAI 69
MANHATTAN 38
MARGARITA 88
MARTINI 116
MATADOR 92
MAYAN 94
METROPOLITAN 17
MEXICAN MULE 108
MEXICANO 111
MEXICO CITY 98
MILIONAIRE'S MARTINI 132
MOJITO 63
MONKEY WRENCH 84
MONTREAL 39
NAGARA FALLS 26
NEGRONI 118
New Yorker 40
NIGHTMARE MARTINI 135
OLD CUBAN 76

OLD FASHIONED 36
OLD FRIEND 130
ORANGE BLOOSOM 122
PAINKILLER 82
PEDRO COLLINS 83
PENICILIN 49
PINA COLADA 68
PLAYA DEL MAR 95
POLISH MARTINI 33
PORNSTAR MARTINI 10
PORTOFINO 31
PURSUIT OF HAPPINESS 53
RAFAELLO 25
RED HOOKER 104
RUM SOUR 75
RUSTY NAIL 59
SCREAMING ORGASM 32
SEX ON THE BEACH 12
SHARK BITE 81
STILLETO 54
SUNSHINE COCKTAIL 67
TENNESSEE FIRE BEER 43
TENNESSEE ICED TEA 48
TEQUILA SOUR 89
TEQUILA SUNRISE 87
THE LAST WORD 137
TOM COLLINS 113
ULTIMA PALABRA 97
VAMPIRO 91
VESPER MARTINI 23
VODKA COLLINS 19
VODKA SOUR 11
VOODO 70
WHISKHEY SOUR 35
WHISKY MAC 55
WHITE RUSSIAN 14
ZOMBIE 71

THANK YOU

Thank you for sharing this adventure into the world of cocktails!

I'd love it if you'd share your opinion about my book on amazon.com - thank you very much in advance!

As you may have noticed, no non-alcoholic cocktails were featured in the publication - however, I have a gift for you! If you would like to receive 20 recipes for delicious non-alcoholic cocktails, I invite you to contact me at this email:

lukefaronbooks@gmail.com

Printed in Great Britain
by Amazon

83404917R00086